HISTORY OF SARATOGA

AND THE

BURGOYNE CAMPAIGN

OF 1777.

AN ADDRESS

BY GEN. EDWARD F. BULLARD,

OF SARATOGA SPRINGS.

Delivered at Schuylerville, N. Y., July 4, 1876.

PRICE, 25 CENTS.

BALLSTON SPA, N. Y.
PUBLISHED BY WATERBURY & INMAN.
1876.

HISTORY OF SARATOGA

AN ADDRESS

BY GEN. EDWARD F. BULLARD,

OF SARATOGA SPRINGS.

Delivered at Schuylerville, N. Y., July 4, 1876.

PRICE, 25 CENTS.

BALLSTON SPA, N. Y.
PUBLISHED BY WATERBURY & INMAN.
1876.

HISTORY OF SARATOGA

An Address by Gen. Edward F. Bullard, delivered at Schuylerville, July 4th, 1875.

We are assembled this Fourth day of July, 1876, in pursuance to the joint resolution of Congress, and the president's proclamation, which recommends that the people assemble this day in their several towns and cause to have delivered a historical sketch of such town from its foundation, and that one copy thereof be filed in the clerk's office of the county, and another be filed in the office of the librarian of congress, to the intent that a complete record may be obtained of the progress of our institutions during the first century of their existence.

Standing as we do on ground made historical, and almost sacred, as the place where the British army under Burgoyne surrendered, October 17, 1777, the time allotted us might be made interesting, if we should dwell upon the events of that immortal campaign. But it is due to history, as well as to carry out the resolution of Congress, that we should go somewhat into detail in regard to the early history of this particular locality. It is a remarkable coincidence that eastern New York should have been discovered from different directions, by hostile interests, during the same year (1609), about two hundred and sixty-seven years ago. From the north by the river St. Lawrence, Samuel Champlain, under authority of the French, entered the lake, since bearing his name, and was the first white man who is known to have set foot upon our northern boundaries, which occurred on the 4th day of July, 1609. From the south, the gallant Hendrik Hudson sailed up the bay, and landed upon Manhattan Island on the second day of September, of the same year, and in the name of Protestant Holland, took possession of the place destined to be the great metropolis of the western world. Although Columbus had made his discoveries in 1492, or about one hundred and eleven years earlier, yet this portion of the great continent remained unknown until the voyages of Champlain and Hudson. Excepting the valley of the lower Hudson, what is now the Empire State, with its vast domain, remained unknown for many years later. In November, 1856 President Fillmore exhibited to me at his residence in Buffalo, a very old map, which he had then recently found during his travels in Germany. It is to be regretted that we cannot at this time give the date of it, but its face will give intrinsic evidence of its antiquity. Upon that map, what is known as Lake Ontario was brought down to a point near where Utica is now located, and Mohawk river is marked as its outlet. From the junction of the Mohawk and Hudson, down to the Atlantic, it was exceedingly correct, while it was evident that all north and west of that point had been made by conjecture, upon information probably obtained from the natives. The north, or main branch of the river was laid down as the outlet of what is now known as Saratoga lake, without dreaming that our noble Hudson had its sources over a hundred miles further north in the forests of the majestic Adirondacks. It is thus evident that Saratoga lake, its outlet (Fish Creek) and the river below that point, were regarded as places of great importance by the aborigines of that period. As the streams afforded the only natural highways of the country, the Hudson, lakes George and Champlain, were the routes by which all communication was had between the hostile settlements. As Saratoga was about half way between New York and the St. Lawrence river, this place has witnessed the passage of the early pioneer, as well as the hostile bands of the seventeenth century. Every war between England and France and every revolution in England which affected its ruling monarch, reached this country and embroiled the savage tribes.

The fertility of her soil, the beauty of her scenery, and the utility of her great water courses and falls, early attracted the sagacious and enterprising European. Hence as early as November 4th, 1684, we find that the natives had given a title to an immense tract of land upon both sides of the river, to Peter Schuyler and others. About three years later, 1687, we find that Dongan the royal governor of this colony, had been in negotiation with certain Mohawk converts, then in Canada, to induce them to return, and they were willing to do so upon condition that he would secure to them a location at "Serachtague," described as lying upon the Hudson river, about forty miles above Albany, evidently including the place where we now stand. It will thus be seen that those intelligent aborigines selected this beautiful country in preference to their former native Mohawk valley. From this time onward, for the next century, this locality was destined to be the great battle ground between the opposing forces of civilization, which were then contending for the mastery of the human race. At this period no district, town or county had been organized under the name of Saratoga, but the whole country along the river, on each side to a considerable distance, was known under that general name.

In the winter of 1690 the French and Indians came up Lake Champlain and Lake George and passed through this district near what is now the village of Saratoga Springs, on their way to destroy Schenectady.

In the year 1693 another force of French and Indians came south over nearly the same route nntil they reached the gap or canyon in the mountain at what is now known as Stiles, in Wilton, about ten miles northwest of this place and about five miles northeast of Saratoga Springs, when they turned west and passed over to the Mohawk valley, where they destroyed the forts of those Indians friendly to the English. On their return they were pursued by these Indians with a force under Schuyler, from Albany, and overtaken at the Stiles place, where the French built a temporary fort and where a sanguinary battle ensued, when the enemy hastily retreated. This is the first important battle between the French and English that we find recorded in history as having occurred in the Saratoga district. It was nearly two centuries ago and nearly a century before the mineral springs were known to the white race. These raids and wars continued to disturb this locality until about the year

1700.

Soon after the opening of the eighteenth century the English government, to form a barrier against the French, saw the importance of planting a colony as far north as practicable upon the upper Hudson river. This no doubt induced the government to confirm the Indian title of 1684. The governor of Canada in a letter to the king of France, Feb. 13 1731, ascribes that motive to the English for conferring this grant upon certain influential residents of Orange (Albany). Hence we find that the first legal title to the land here from a civilized government was granted October 29, 1708, by Lord Cornbury, the governor of this colony, to Peter Philip Schuyler, Robert Livingston, Derick Wessells, John Johnson Bleecker, Johannes Schuyler, and Cornelius Van Dyck. It began on the west side of the Hudson river, at the south side of the mouth of the creek called "Tionooudehowee," (now at the village of Mechanicville) and extended north to the mouth of the creek on the east side of the Hudson river, called "Dionoondehowee," (now called the Batten-Kill) about one mile north of Schuylerville, and extending six miles to each side of the river, except that the portion on the east side of the river was bounded south by the Hoosac patent. In the patent it was estimated to be about twenty two miles north and south, but when it was Surveyed by a straight line it was only about seventeen miles long. Thus it will be seen, that these six purchasers obtained a princely estate of about 204 square miles, or over one hundred and thirty thousand acres of the finest land on the continent. It included the most of the present towns of Saratoga and Stillwater, in the county of Saratoga, and the town of Easton in the present county of Washington. As near as we can learn from history and tradition, the Schuylers, soon after 1708, erected buildings near what is now known as Schuylerville, and induced some tenants to remain as permanent settlers. About the year 1709 a military road was constructed from Batten-Kill on the east side of the river to Fort Edward and thence to Whitehall, a distance of about forty miles. As the river was navigable from Stillwater rapids north to the Batten-Kill, about 12 miles, most of the travel here was by water, and the landing for the north to connect with the new road was on the east side of the river, it is evident that the village in the early part of the last century was partly on that side of the river.

In 1709, Col. Schuyler built a fort about a mile northeast of the place where we now stand. It was located on the east side of the river on the second highland south of the mouth of the Batten-Kill in what was then Saratoga, but now in the county of Washington, and was upon the farm now occupied by Simon Sheldon, whose ancestors have occupied the same about a century. It is probable that the Schuylers did not become *permanent* residents here as early as that period, as we find that Philip, (afterwards major-general) was born in Albany in 1731. We find, however, that in 1745, Capt. Peter Schuyler was a permanent resident here, and his house was on the west side of the river just south of the present village bearing the family name, and about thirty rods south of Fish Creek and about the same distance east of the famous Schuyler mansion, built soon after 1777 and now owned and occupied by George Strover, Esq. The governor of Canada in the same letter of the 13th day of February, 1731 to the king of France, proposed to build a fort upon lake Champlain at Crown Point, and submitted with it a map of that lake and of the Hudson river called by him the Orange river. The only places of sufficient military importance to be named on that map, were Manathe (New York) Orange (Albany) Sarahtogua, and the great carrying place (Fort Edward). Although that was 122 years after Champlain had made his discoveries, yet the French engineer who made that map supposed the Mohawk river joined the Hudson west of Glen's Falls, and it is so laid down on his map and so treated in the governor's dispatch. He proposes to build the fort at Crown Point as a convenient point from which to harass the English as they had from 1689, to 1699. To carry out that plan we find that in November, 1745, and about thirty-two years before Burgoyne's surrender, the village then called Saratoga was destroyed by the French and Indians. In Lossing's history of the Schuyler family he makes the date November 28th, but in Stone's history of the life and times of Sir William Johnson he put the date at November 17th, and the latter would seem to be the more reliable date, as the massacre was the cause of an angry dispute between George Clinton, then governor, and the colonial assembly then in session at New York, and the records of that assembly show that it adjourned November 28th. At that period it was evident that this was the extreme outpost of the English on the frontier. The village consisted of about thirty families and one hundred and fifty persons, many of whom were slaves. As the fort was then on the east side of the river there can be no reasonable doubt that the main part of the village was yet on the same side of the river, although the Schuyler residence and some of the mills were on the west side. This attack was made by the Indians and French at the dead hour of night, without warning, and many persons killed and 109 captured and taken to Canada. The fort was destroyed; every house burned, and every building except one saw mill which was not discovered. We have not been able to locate that mill, but judging from circumstances it must have been on the Batten-Kill about half a mile up stream and east of the Hudson river where the Clark's Mills now stand. Capt. Schuyler was killed in his own house while bravely defending himself, as were many others. We have not space for more details. The same horror which had occurred at Schenectady, fifty-five years earlier, (1690) was re-enacted here in November 1745. This Captain Peter Schuyler, who then lost his life, was an uncle of Gen Phillip Schuyler, whose buildings were burned by Burgoyne 32 years later. The first was fighting against the French to maintain the supremacy of the English on this continent, while the latter was in the cause of the colonies, attempting to overthrow that same English supremacy and establish an independent republic. The old Schuyler residence which was burned in 1745, stood within the lines of the present Champlain canal, and when the same was enlarged and widened to the west within a few years past, the excavation revealed the remains of the old chimney and fire-place, some of the relics of which are yet preserved. In 1746, the fort on the east side of the river, was rebuilt by order cf the legislature, and was mainly constructed of logs and timber, on the heights overlooking the river, and it was then named Fort Clinton in honor of the governor. This fort should not be confounded with the entrenchments, thrown up in 1777, further south, and opposite Schuylerville, which the Americans made to cut off the retreat of Burgoyne.

In the year 1746 the war on this frontier continued. On the 13th day of May of than year, as three men belonging to the garrison of Saratoga were fishing near the fort, they were surprised by Indians, who killed a son of William Norwood and took a German prisoner, while the third escaped to the fort. On the 15th day of December of the same year, we find in the newspapers of New York, it was published that the Indians lately killed four men and took four others prisoners at Saratoga. Capt. Schuyler, in command of the militia here, went out to their assistance, but came near being cut off, and with difficulty retreated to the fort. At this time the fort was occupied in part by some New Jersey troops. On the 12th day of October, 1746, at Saratoga, sixteen men were killed and taken about a mile from the fort. They belonged to Langdon's and Hart's companies. There were about one hundred and fifty Indians when they attacked a party guarding some wagons on the west side of the river south of Fish Creek.

In the year 1747 the war continued more sanguinary than ever along the borders. On the 7th day of April of that year the French and Indians under the command of M. de St. Luc to the number of 200 attacked Capt. Trent and Lieut. Proctor as they were passing along the river near the ruins of Capt. Schuyler's house. They were ambushed, and eight of their men killed and several wounded. In the meantime Capt. Livingston dispatched Capt. Bradt with a company from the fort on the east side of the river, to reinforce the party on the west side, when the enemy hastily retreated to the wilderness. Shortly before June 15 of that year a force of about 200 French and Indians made another attack on the fort, but it held out until reinforcements under Col. Schuyler arrived from Albany, when the enemy again retreated. About this time many raids from Canada penetrated as far as Massachusetts and Connecticut, where villages were burned, the innocent massacreed and others brought back as captives. The route from Canada for those hostile incursions frequently led near here, leaving the river at the mouth of the Batten-Kill and passing thence southeasterly to New England. On the return of those hostile bands, many a weary captive has been led up this valley and in many narratives and letters giving an account of their hardships the familiar name of Saratoga appears.

Thus the war which was begun in 1744 continued. The few inhabitants of this frontier were in continual alarm. During this period Sir William Johnson came up from Albany with an army, and passed this point, but did not meet any large force of the enemy and returned. As soon as any large force was withdrawn, the defenceless inhabitants would again be left exposed to the tomahawk. In the feeble state of the colony, the authorities concluded that fall to abandon this post, and the stores and ammunition were then transported back to Albany, and the fort burned December 1, 1747. From that time forward, for some years, this whole country was abandoned to the French and Indians, and Albany was the northern English outpost. The English under Gen. Lyman built a fort on the north side of Fish Creek at its confluence with the Hudson in August, 1755, which is only a few rods from where we are now assembled. The road now leading to the bridge crossing the river runs directly through it. Nelson in his work, and also French's Gazetteer of 1860 of our state, by mistake asserts that this fort was built by the French. Its name "Fort Hardy" is conclusive evidence of its English origin as Sir Charles Hardy was then governor of that colony, It is another remarkable coincidence, that only 22 years later the army of Burgoyne, in 1777, laid down their arms within this very fort, to the patriotic Americans, then struggling for their freedom. Notwithstanding these troublous times, during the year 1750, John R. Bleecker made a survey of the Saratoga patent for the owners, and divided it into twenty-eight great lots about one-half of a mile wide, extending six miles west from the river, which, at the southwest corner about reaches the present site of the camp meeting grounds, near Round Lake, and at the northwest, extending about one mile north of Stafford's bridge. It was also surveyed into subdivisions by cross lines, and the owners stood ready to give leases or deeds to those who dare venture into this hostile territory. Very few, however, would risk their lives at this early period, as this ever continued to be the great highway for the passage of hostile armies. Late in 1755 the English, under Sir William Johnson, at Lake George, after a sanguinary battle, defeated the French under the celebrated Dieskau, which for the time, held the enemy in check. Only two years later, (1757), the French, under Montcalm, recaptured Lake George, and massacred the brave Colonel Monroe and his army, who had but a few months before passed through here on his way to the north. Only a year later Abercrombie passed here with an army of 16,000 men on his way to Lake George and Ticonderoga, where, on the 8th day of July, 1758 he suffered the terrible repulse, well known to all students of history.*

*Those with the Scotch portion of the British army, made the attack, and so bravely cut their way through the abattis. For hours they withstood the terrible fire of the French musketry without the ability to return it with effect. Night coming on, Abercrombie, who had not been within miles of the battle, called off the troops, and commenced his retreat to Albany. Colonel Fitch with his colonial regiments covered the retreat of the regulars very much in the same manner that Washington did at Braddock's defeat.

With and comprising a portion of that army were sixteen colonial regiments under the command of the senior Colonel, Thomas Fitch.*

The next year Gen. Amherst with an army of 12,000 men again left Albany and passed here on his way to retrieve the losses of the year previous, and in July, 1759, he took possession of Ticonderoga and Crown Point without resistance on the part of the French. The capture of Quebec in September, 1759, by the brave Gen. Wolf, ended the most sanguinary fighting of this seven year's war. During that period, commouly called the French war, the great majority of the troops were furnished by New England. Her people did not feel that any peace would long continue while Lake Champlain was under control of a hostile power. Southern New England was then an old settled country, compared with New York. The small colony of Connecticut furnished more troops than New York. The following is from an old Lieutanant's commission now in the possession of a citizen of this countv, dated March 23, 1759, given to John Caltorn, under the hand and seal of "Thomas Fitch, Esq., Captain-General and Governor-in-Chief, in and over his Majesty's English colony of Connecticut, in New England, America." The commission was in a regiment of foot, raised "for invading Canada, and carrying war into the heart of the enemy's possessions." The treaty between the English and French signed at Fontainbleau, France, February 10, 1763, by which all of Canada was ceded to England, for a time gave peace to this distracted locality. During the next ten years, bold pioneers from New England and southern New York began to settle in this vicinity. As yet, all of this locality was called Saratoga, extending south to Mechanicville, and north to the river, and included what is now Saratoga Springs. Before 1770, we find permanently settled within this territory John Strover, on the farm now owned by James Bailey, Esq.; James Brisbin upon the farm now owned by his grandson, James C. Brisbin, and Conrad Cramer upon the farm now occupied by John Smith, about three miles southwest of Schuylerville. The latter was an enterprising German, who emigrated to this country when young, and left four sons, of whom George, Conrad and John afterwards were member of the legislature of the state of New York. Jesse Mott, a Quaker, resided upon the farm a short distance east of Dean's Corners; Stephen Viele upon the Wagman farm, and Hezekiah Dunham upon the farm now owned by Hiram Cramer. Next to Gen. Schuyler, the latter was the most active patriot in his section. Thomas Smith, the ancestor of several of your townsmen, resided on the hill where Stephen Smith, his grandson, now resides.

Among the names made famous in this locality by all of the writers upon the campaign of Burgoyne is Dovegat. It signifies a cove or bay of water. It in fact represeuts a bay about seventy feet wide of deep water extending about a mile northwest from the river into which a small stream empties. It is about three miles south of Schuylerville, and as the bridges at that point were destroyed, the British and American armies were brought to a halt at that place. It is now known as Coveville and the farm on the north side is now occupied by Charles H. Sarle. Among the residents south of that point mentioned by Baron Reidesel in 1777, was a man named Sword, whose house was near Van Buren's Ferry, where Robert Sarle now resides, about six miles south of Schuylerville. Within that part of Saratoga, afterwards set off as Stillwater, there were settlements made before 1770, among which were George Palmer. and also the Thompsons. March 24,1772, the colonial legislature first passed an act organizing this territory into a legal entity. What is now Saratoga county, was then divided into two districts, "Halfmoon" and "Saraghtoga." As there were no towns then organized here, the Saraghtoga district included Easton, now in the county of Washington, and nearly all the present county of Saratoga north of Anthony's Kill, which enters the Hudson river at Mechanicville, and so continued until April 1, 1775, when the west part of the county was organized into a separate district called Ball's Town. As there was no law requiring deeds to be recorded and no place to do so, except with the secretary of state, or county clerk, at Albany, but few can be found, and hence the difficulty of tracing the name or location of settlers before that time. After the division of the district, April 1, 1775, as before stated, Saraghtoga yet included Easton, and all of the present county of Saratoga, which is now known as Stillwater, Malta, Saratoga, Northumberland, Moreau, Wilton, Saratoga Springs and the eastern portions of Greenfield and Corinth, and so continued until March 7, 1788. The west line of this old Saratoga district ran through near what is now called Greenfield Centre. When therefore we are reading of the great events which occurred between those dates, and which covered the whole period of the revolutionary war, they must be interpreted with these descripions in view, to make history intelligible. We have now briefly given the history of the first century, and which brings us down to

July 4, 1776.

Time will not allow us to treat of the great questions agitating two continents, which led to the immortal declaration enunciated at Philadelphia just one century ago. A brief narrative of the great events which had their centre here, is all that the resolution of congress contemplated. These are so important, that the historian has already immortalized nearly every detail, and we might content ourselves by referring the reader to the Memoirs of Gen. James Wilkinson, published in 1816; History of New York, by Dunlap; History of the war of the Independence of the United States, by Botta; the life and times of Sir William Johnson; Memoirs of Gen. Reidesel, also of Madame Reidesel; and also, Reminiscences of Saratoga, by William L. Stone, and Sketches of Northern New York, by N. B. Sylvester, which contain very full accounts of that romantic campaign. As, however, time is fast obliterating many of the old landmarks, your speaker, (a native of this village) has endeavered to aid in locating and interpreting some of them for the benefit of future generations. About June 18, 1776, congress appointed

Gen. Gates to the command of the army of the north and made him dictator in Canada for six months. On the 16th day of July, 1776, we find that Gates was in command at Ticonderoga, and during that whole season, stirring times were had on the Champlain and in its vicinity. All of the troops and supplies passed here on their way north, mostly carried upon batteaux, navigated up the river. Within six years past, a shell was found in the river about a mile south of Schuylerville which is fully eight inches in diameter, and which probably was lost overboard while being transported, within the century ending October 1777. In the spring of 1777, Gen Schuyler arrived at Albany and assumed the command of the northern department. June 20, we find he was at Ticonderoga. About that time Burgoyne commenced his movement from Montreal, expecting to sunder the colonies and put an end to the rebellion. July 4, 1777, Gen. Burgoyne took possession of Mount Defiance, which commanded Ticonderoga, and which compelled our army to evacuate that place a few days later. At Whitehall, then called Skeensborough, Burgoyne issued a proclamation to the people offering pardon, and calling upon the people to send a delegation of ten from each town to meet at Castleton, (Vermont), July 15. In the meantime, the remnant of our army reached Fort Edward, where on the 13th day of July, Gen. Schuyler issued a counter proclamation. The British pressed on, and our army was obliged to retreat, and on the 28th day of July, 1777, it was encamped at Moses Kill about eight miles north of this place. Gen. Schuyler on that day, wrote a letter to Gen. Washington, dated at "Saratoga." July 30, our army moved from Moses Kill to Schuylerville, and after halting here a few days, on the second day of August, proceeded to Stillwater. On the 12th day of August, while their main force remained at Fort Miller a detachment of the British marched from the north side of the Batten-Kill for Bennington, where on the 16th, it was repulsed by our brave New Englanders, under General Stark. This success gave great confidence to our cause and induced recruits to hurry forward, and join Schuyler's army upon the Hudson. On the 10th of September the advance portion of the British army crossed from the east side of the Hudson river to the west of it, about two miles north of Schuylerville. At that place the river could be forded upon the rapids until within a short distance of the west shore, where a short bridge was constructed across a deep, narrow channel in the rocks. The point where the army left the bridge is upon the farm now owned by Daniel A. Bullard, and the excavation through the embankment is yet plainly visible, and will long remain a monument of that event. The British army made a short tarry here and their advanced posts threw up intrenchments from near the site of the present Reformed church, extending southerly along near the present residence of Charles W. Mayhew. August 11, Gen. Schuyler left Stillwater, and on the 18th, posted his army on Van Schaick's Island at the mouth of the Mohawk river, being the first island south of Waterford. In a military view, Schuyler's leaving Stillwater was regarded by congress as a mistake, and hence Gen. Gates was appointed to supercede him and he arrived and assumed command August 19. That island, as a place of defense was a natural Gibraltar, being of triangular shape, with high perpendicular rock embankments nearly around it. Upon the Northeast corner intrenchments were thrown up which are yet visible as we pass in the cars near the south end of the bridge. If Burgoyne had reached that point, he could have crossed the Mohawk a few miles further west and waited the arrival of the British army then coming up the Hudson, and being thus reinforced, could have surrounded the American army with a prospect of success. In that strong position the British could not, with safety assault this island, but by taking possession of the high ground west of Waterford and north of Cohoes, could have commanded the position, the same as Mount Defiance had commanded Ticonderoga but a few months previous to that time. Knowing the condition of affairs as they were subsequently ascertained, it was evidently a wise move to march the American army back to the high lands in Stillwater, a short distance north from Bemis Heights, and about 15 miles north of the Mohawk and twenty-five miles distant from Albany. The position thus selected lay between the Hudson river on the east and Saratoga lake only six miles to the west; the high lands west of the river valley were cut by three deep ravines leading easterly, forming strong natural barriers against an approaching army; the whole country in this vicinity was a wilderness, and the high ground approaches so near the river there, that it was the most advantageous point in the whole valley to dispute the passage of the British army moving from the north. Such was the place selected by the experienced Polish patriot Kosciusko, and approved by Gen. Gates, as the Thermopylea of the struggle for American freedom.

Gen. Schuyler was a pure man—a true patriot, a man of great sagacity and good judgment. Of course he acted from the best knowledge of facts that he could then obtain. Gen. Washington had probably better means of knowing the condition of general affairs, and it was not surprising, therefore, that he saw the error of Schuyler, and directed Gates to lead the army further back into the wilderness. This position brought the armies face to face; the small stream emptying into the river at Wilbur's Basin being between them. Circumstances would necessarily soon bring on a conflict, and the sanguinary battle of September 19 followed. Both parties claimed the victory, but it mas not decisive. The scene of that battle was on Freeman's farm, about eight miles from Schuylerville, a little to the west of south, and about ten miles southeast of Saratoga Springs. As the American army was daily growing stronger, and the British weaker, the latter could not long remain inactive, and the battle of October 7 followed upon nearly the same ground where the former had taken place. The engagement resulted in a substantial victory for our cause, and compelled the British to attempt an escape by a retreat to the north. Their army reached this village about October 10, pursued closely by Gen. Gates. Schuyler had made a mistake two months earlier, as we have seen, by moving his army too far south. So now Gen. Gates made a mistake, which if the British had taken advantage of it, might have changed the final result. Anticipating a retreat by the British army about Oct. 6, Gates dispatched Gen. Fellows with 1,500 men on the east side of the river to pass north and cut off the retreat. They proceeded on the east side and across the Batten-Kill where they they should have remained for safety. But they were ordered to cross the river at that point, and did so, (at the same ford where Burgoyne had crossed a month earlier,) and took position on the high lands west of that ford, less than two miles north of Schuylerville. While there one night a British regiment under Lieut. Col. Southerland marched around the American camp without being discovered, and he urged Burgoyne to attack them. Fortunately for our cause Burgoyne hesitated, and the next day Gen. Gates corrected the mistake and ordered Fellows to recross the river and take position upon the north of the Batten Kill, where he remained until Burgoyne's surrender. If Burgoyne had captured that detachment of the American army his way of retreat would have been open and the experienced Gen. Reidesel felt assured that the British army could reach the lakes in safety where an abundance of vessels and supplies could have easily been obtained. Thus at times upon a single breath seemes to rest the great events which are to determine the future of nations.

A month earlier, on the way south, the British had erected earth works on the east side of the river opposite Schuylerville, to hold back the American reinforcement coming from the east. The Americans now took possession of the same intrenchments, faced them to the west, and poured a continual fire upon the enemy posted where is now the present village of Schuylerville. What was known as the village then, and was called Saratoga, according to contemporary writers, consisted of about thirty isolated houses on the south side of Fish creek. The old Dutch reformed church then stood about one-third of a mile south of Fish creek, on the side hill west of the present turnpike road and just south of the road leading westerly to Victory. That church was then used by the British as a hospital, and as we now learn from George Strover, a young woman who was setting by a window in the church, eating an apple, was instantly killed by a rifle shot from the American army. About this time Burgoyne occupied the Gen. Schuyler residence for his headquarters for a single night; but the approach of the American forces drove him from there, and he next located his headquarters in the centre of his camp, probably a short distance west of the new and elegant school edifice on the heights overlooking this beautiful landscape. Until the surrender, his army remained here and threw up entrenchments, facing the southeast, extending nearly as far back as the new cemetery, and thence extending south on the same elevation towards Victory Mills. The barracks used for a hospital were on a farm now owned by Alanson Welch at the north end of the village. The house now owned by the family of the late William B. Marshall, about one mile further north, is yet standing, and was then occupied for the time being by the ladies who accompanied the English, and by the wounded officers of their army. Madame Reidesel, one of the most heroic female characters of any age, was with her husband during this period, and in her contemporaneous letters, written to her friends in Germany, has recorded most faithfully the romantic incidents of that eventful campaign, and immortalized the house which yet stands as a monument of those times. In her letters she stated that under the house "were three beautiful cellars. I proposed that the most dangerously wounded of the officers should be brought into one of them; that the women should remain in another, and that all the rest should stay in the third, which was nearest the entrance. I had just cleansed the cellars, when a fresh and terrible cannonade threw us all once more into alarm * * * my children were already under the cellar steps, * * eleven cannon balls went through the house, and we could plainly hear them rolling over our heads. One poor soldier, (Surgeon Jones), whose leg they were about to amputate, having been laid upon a table for this purpose, had the other leg taken off by another cannon ball in the very middle of the operation. His comrades all ran off, and when they again came back they found him in one corner of the room, where he had rolled in anguish, scarcely breathing." The Americans had taken possession of the highlands north of Batten-Kill, about three quarters of a mile northeast of this house, and from that point these balls were mainly fired. The one which killed Surgeon Jones entered the front parlor at the northeast corner, and passed through the plank forming the partition on the south side of the room, the particular plank hit standing west of the south door. This shows conclusively that the cannon were fired from a point north of the Batten-Kill. At that time this house belonged to the Lansing family, of Albany, and was probably occupied by them as a summer residence. It was deserted before the British army arrived from the north in September. It was a two story house, having a gable or French roof, fronting east with a hall in the middle and a room at each end. The modern historian (writing in 1877) is mistaken when he says, "the house was allowed to fall to decay a few years since." On the contrary, it was merely improved by putting on a new flat roof and making the cellar still deeper. One of the old rafters and the plank of the partition, each shattered by a cannon ball, are still carefully preserved on the spot by Mrs. Marshall. She has kindly placed in my hands a gold piece, found by Samuel Marshall on those premises abont fifty years ago, which is stamped, "Georgius III., *Dei Gratia*," with his profile on the one side, and on the other the British crown, 1776. This was evidently a coin lost by the officers in 1777.* A Mr. Willard, residing near the foot of the mountain opposite the battle ground, by night would display signals from its top by different lights, in such manner as from time to time to give the Americans the location and movements of the British army. That mountain is plainly visible from Albany and Fort Edward. It has ever since been known by the name of "Willard's mountain." That is certainly one of the earliest systems of telegraphing known to have been put in practice. To return to events of October, 1777. As Burgoyne abandoned the south side of Fish creek, he caused the residence of Gen. Schuyler and his mills to be burned. That residence was located about sixty feet further south than the present one,

---

*The whole country in this vicinity was strewn with relics. About the year 1850 Ebenezer Leggett while excavating for a barn upon the Freeman farm found several hundred dollars in gold among human remains, apparently carried in belts.

and the ancient lilac bushes then in the rear garden, are yet standing near the canal. The mills were upon the north side of the creek, near the same spot where Bullard's flouring mill now stands. At that time there was no village north of Fish creek, and only one or two buildings besides the mills and barracks, so far as can be ascertained from history or tradition. Gen. Gates' army was then mainly stationed upon the highlands south of Fish creek, extending up to a point opposite Victory Mills. As an army of six thousand men in a locality almost a wilderness, could not draw many new supplies in a hostile country, matters were soon brought to a crisis by the surrender of the whole British Army, October 17, 1777. The privates stacked their arms, etc., within the lines of old Fort Hardy, on the north side of Fish creek, upon yonder flat, a few rods below where we stand.* Burgoyne and his officers crossed over Fish creek in company with Adjutant Wilkinson, of Gen. Gates' staff, and were presented to Gen. Gates. Gen. Wilkinson afterwards wrote an account of it, from which we extract: "Gen. Gates, advised of Burgoyne's approach, met him at the head of his camp; Burgoyne, in a rich royal uniform, and Gates in a plain blue frock. When they approached nearly within sword's length they reined up and halted. I then named the gentlemen, and Gen. Burgoyne raised his hat most gracefully, said: 'The fortune of war, Gen. Gates, has made me your prisoner.' To which the conqueror, returning a courtly salute, promptly replied: 'I shall always be ready to bear testimony that it has not been through any fault of your Excellency.'" As near as we are now able to locate the head quarters of Gen. Gates they were near the spring on the west side of the turnpike about half a mile south of Fish creek.†

The importanee of this event, even at the end of a century, cannot be fully comprehended. Eminent authorities have pronounced it one of the

---

*Since this address was delivered E. R. Mann of Ballston Spa, who is well versed in American history,has called my attention to the STARS AND STRIPES which we claim to be natives of old Saratoga.

The flag was adopted by congress, June 14, 1777, and on the 10th day of September 1777 was first announced to our army as the emblem of the young nation. The ladies at once made a banner with the thirteen stars, which was displayed at the head of Gates' army. On the 17th day of October, 1777 it here first waved in triumph over an American army and was thereby consecrated to the cause of liberty.

†Our favorite Yankee Doodle was also here first adopted as the hymn of freedom. Although some four verses of it were composed by a British surgeon about twenty years earlier at East Albany to redicule the Connecticut brigade which then appeared under Col. Thomas Fitch, we do not find that it was ever adopted by our side earlier than October 1777. After the British army had stacked their arms in Fort Hardy October 17, they crossed Fish creek and passed south through the long lines of the America army. As our victorious host did not feel like insulting a fallen foe it was suggested that a lively tune be played for their consolation, and by common consent, the melodious Yankee Doodle was given by the whole American lines, while the rank and file of the British were passing between them. Unless some other locality shall prove an older title, you can justly claim that our famous Yankee Doodle, was first sung in this valley, as the national tune of free America. The 4th Connecticut regiment did gallant service in the Revolu-

greatest battles known in human history, when measured by its far reaching consequences.‡

As a result of this success in December 1777, France made a treaty with our commissioners recognizing the independent character of the United States, which in that instance amounted practically to a declaration of war against England, and France soon gave national aid to our cause. It was the first great success of the people struggling for self-government against the prestige of king craft and despotism. It has been well said, that without this result at Saratoga, Bunker Hill would have been insignificant and York town an impossibility. Great and crushing as was the defeat at Saratoga, the war was not yet ended, and the struggle continued for five years longer. Nor did this locality escape the trials and hardships of those times which tried men's souls. The march and counter march of this hostile army with its barbarous allies, had completely desolated the whole region hereabouts. This county had been richly laden with the golden harvest and domestic animals for the use of the husbandman. As a specimen, the farm of James Brisbin had sufficient wheat and cattle to have paid the purchase price, but it was all taken and consumed by Burgoyne's army without compensation, notwithstanding the fair promises made in his proclamation of July 10, before stated. We should except a single cow, which escaped from her captors, returned home and was afterwards secreted and saved. After the surrender, the farmers gradually returned to their rural homes, erected new log houses, and began again to till the soil. But little progress, however, was made, as this valley lay in the track of the Indians and tories, who had fled to Canada, and made repeated raids into this county. Such murderous incursions were made in May, 1779, in this locality; October 6, 1780, when Gen. Gordon and a large number of citizens of Ballston and Milton were

---

tionary war at White Plains, Trenton and Saratoga, and Andrew Fitch, a son of Col, Thomas Fitch was a Lieut. Col. in that regiment and probably had the pleasure of hearing that tune under different circumstances, from those under which his father had heard it in derision twenty years earlier.

‡Hallam, the celebrated historian of the middle ages, in speaking of the decisive battles defines them as "those few battles, of which a contrary event would have essentially varied the drama of the world in all its subsequent scenes." An eminent English authority, E. S. Crecy professor of ancient and modern history in the university college, London as late as 1851, selected what he deemed as the fifteen decisive battles of the world, beginning with the battle of Marathon which occurred 2366 years ago, and ending with Waterloo which was fought in 1815. Among those fifteen great battles, this English author includes SARATOGA. In speaking of it, he says: "Nor can any military event be said to have exercised more important influence on the future fortunes of mankind than the complete defeat of Burgoyne's expedition in 1777." * * * "When the news of the capture of Ticonderoga by the British army July 4, 1777, reached Paris, the American commissioners in despair, had almost broken off all negotation with France, and they endeavored to open communication with England, in which they were not successful, but when the news of Saratoga reached Paris, the whole scene was changed. Franklin and his brother commisssioners found all of their difficulties with the French government vanished."

carried as captives to Canada; 1781, when Joe Bettys, the Ballston tory, the second time appeared at Ballston and carried away many captives; August 1781, when the tory Waltermire, with his Indian allies, returned as far south as Albany with intent to capture Gen. Schuyler; April 14, 1782, in the southwest part of the county, when Gonzalez and his eldest son were massacred and a son of 14 carried away a captive. The raid of May, 1779, more immediately affected this locality and the few inhabitants, scattered in the interior, fled from it to avoid certain destruction. After the surrender of Burgoyne, Conrad Cramer had returned to his farm, about three miles southwest of here and was living on the borders with his wife and four small children, when, on the 14th day of May, they had to flee for their lives. They hastily packed their wagon with what comforts one team could carry, and started on their flight southerly. They reached the river road and proceeded as far south as the farm now owned by Lohnas, about five miles south of this place, when night overtook them. At that place there was a small house used as a tavern, but as it was already full, the Cramer family were obliged to remain in their wagon, and on that same evening the mother gave birth to a child, (John Cramer), who afterwards became, probably, the most distinguished person ever born in this town.* The next morning the family continued the flight to what is now known as the Fitzgerald neighborhood, about three miles south of Mechanicville, where they obtained a small house, in which they remained until it was considered safe to return to their home in the wilderness. During the Gates campaign John Strover had command of a party of scouts, because he was well acquainted hereabouts. He was present at the execution of Thomas Lovelace, a malignant tory, who was hung upon an oak tree, about thirty rods south of where George Strover now resides. At that date the gravel ridge extended east as far as where the canal now is, and the oak tree stood upon the east point of the gravel ridge near where the store house of the Victory company now stands. When the Waterford and Whitehall turnpike was constructed through there, about 1813, the stump of the old oak was removed by the excavation. John Strover had frequently informed his son George that Lovelace was buried in a standing posture, near the tree. When the excavation took place, George stood by and saw the bones, yet in a standing posture removed from the very spot which had been pointed out by his father. During the campaign Burgoyne employed Lovelace and other tories as spies, and they were generally secreted in the woods between here and Saratoga Lake.† One day Capt. Dunham, then residing near the lake, in company with Daniel Spike and a colored man, was scouring the woods,

---

*When John Cramer was born he weighed less than four pounds and his parents had but little hopes that he could be reared. At manhood he became a very large broad chested large headed man with an iron constitution and a giant intellect. He died at Waterford in this county June 1, 1870, aged 91 years and 16 days.

†About two miles west of Mechanicville on the highland north of Anthony's Kill is a place called Tory Hill. During Burgoyne's campaign

and while crossing upon a tree which had fallen over the brook east of the Wagman farm, discovered five guns stacked in the hiding place of the spies. With a sudden rush, Dunham and his associates seized the guns and captured all five of the spies, bound and brought them into the American camp. We have not been able to give the date of the arrest or execution of Lovelace, but think it was after the close of Burgoyne's campaign.* Gen. Stark was then at Schuylerville and presided at the court martial before which he was tried. With a vindictive tory element in their midst, and the Indians on the borders, but little progress was made in permanently settling this county, until after peace was declared. Although the Springs, eleven miles west of here, had been discovered by the whites, and were visited by Sir. William Johnson in 1767, yet there were but a few log huts, if any there, prior to 1783, when Gen, Schuyler first cut a road from here to the Springs, where he built the first frame building in 1784. After the termination of the revolutionary war, and about 1783, pioneers began more freely to settle in this locality. Gen. Abraham Ten Broeck of Albany, the counsel and guardian of the Patroon Van Rensselaer, had become the owner of a large share of the lands in the Saratoga patent, and he induced persons to locate upon them by giving what was called life leases, at a small annual rent. As a specimen, one is dated June 24, 1783, given to Zopher Scidmore, for three lives, viz: to continue during the life of himself, his wife Mary, and his son David, upon paying a rent of £6 and 16 shillings; containing 136 acres, and being lot 15, in great lot 22. That farm is about six miles southwest of this place. As Virginia was called the mother of states, so Old Saratoga may be called the mother of towns. After the state of New York had became a state government and in running order, on the 7th day of March, 1788, an act was passed organizing towns, instead of districts. By that statute Stillwater, including Malta, was taken off from Saratoga, thus making what is now Sarataga county into four towns, viz: Halfmoon, Saratoga, Ballston and Stillwater, all of which were yet a part of Albany county.

In 1777 there were a few houses at what is now Stillwater village, and as that was the nearest point to the American headquarters some of the dispatches were dated at Stillwater, although that whole territory was then within the Saratoga district. Hence the apparent confusion of calling the battle sometimes by the name of Stillwater and at other times of Saratoga meaning the same place. When Stillwater was taken off as a separate town, she included in her territory the fields upon which the two principal battles were fought. The oldest native of this town now living, of whom we have knowledge, is Hannah (Fitch) Bullard, who was born September 9, 1787, in the eastern part of what is now Greenfield, but was then within the district

---

many of the loyalist secreted themselves in the wilderness there for several weeks. They were regularly supplied with provisions and their camp guarded by pickets. They refused to join the American army and cautiously waited events before going into the British.

*Prof. J. Dorman Steele in his School History of the U. S., gives the date of the execution of Lovelace as December 14, 1779.

of Saratoga. She is present with us to-day, and may God ever bless her.* In 1789 that part of your territory lying east of the Hudson, was taken off from this famous old town and a new one formed called Easton. On the seventh day of February, 1791, this county was cut off from Albany and formed into an independent county, with the name of Saratoga. Before this date Jesse Toll had settled and built a house upon the flats about four miles south of here, upon lands which now belong to Henry C., and George R. Holmes, but as the lands were so low where the house was built, it has been long since removed, and one recently erected on the hill. The records belonging to the old church before the revolution cannot be found, and were probably destroyed during the time it was occupied by the British as a hospital. The date of the oldest church record here now extant is July 10, 1789. There is recorded a meeting of the following persons, choosing to belong to the Reformed Protestant Dutch and Presbyterian church (as it is styled in the record) at that date. At that time it was agreed that the minister to be called should preach the English language. The names of the persons who were associated in the formation of this organization, are as follows: Peter Becker, Abraham Low, John Mahany, Simon De Rider, Corruth Brisbin, Jesse Toll, Julianna Finne, Hendrick Van Buren, Jacobus Abeel, John Smith, John B. Schuyler, Nicholas V. D. Barch, Cornelius McLain, Jacob Dannaeds, Abraham Marshall, Solomon Wheeler, James Brisbin, Stephen Viele, and one or two others. The officers then chosen were elders, Cornelius Van Veghten, Peter Becker; deacons, Jesse Toll, James Abeel. The minister who presided at this meeting was E. Westerlo, who was then settled at Albany. The first pastor was Samuel Smith, who was called the 7th day of October, 1789, who was ordained and installed as their pastor December 10th 1789. At that date the wooden church north of the creek was in process of erection, because of which, it was resolved to have preaching from house to house. December 2, 1791, this church was so far completed that it was resolved, by the consistory, to sell the pews on the second Tuesday of January, 1792. At the above meeting it was resolved, to purchase a parsonage and fifty acres of land. This wooden church was burned January 1, 1831. February 14, 1831, it was resolved to build another house of worship, and a building committee was appointed. The stone church was then erected. The present brick edifice was erected in 1856, and dedicated June 2, 1857. In 1798 this old town was shorn of more of her territory by the organization of Northumberland, which took off all now included in Moreau and Wilton and the east part of Greenfield and Corinth. The Methodist Episcopal church was erected in this place in the year 1825, and the Baptist in 1833. The first Roman Catholic church was erected in the year 1845, which was burned January 22, 1871, and their new beautiful edifice was dedicated October 21, 1873. The Episcopal church was erected

---

*Her father Ebenezer Fitch was a grandson of Gov. Fitch of Connecticut, and served it the war and was at the battle of Stony Point. He moved from Connecticut to Saratoga in 1786.

about the year 1867, a short distance east of Burgoyne's front entrenchment. In 1812 this locality again witnessed the pomp and ceremony of war, as our troops destined for lower Canada and Lake Champlain, from time to time passed here, making short halts on their way north. At that time, the Schuyler mills had been rebuilt and a very small number of other buildings erected north of Fish creek, upon the site of the present village. At that time, as we are now informed by persons then residing here, there were not to exceed ten buildings on the site of your present flourishing village. There was one tavern, kept by Patterson, where the Schuylerville house now stands. The old cemetery was then on the west side of Broadway, north of Burgoyne street, and south of that tavern. At that time there was but one store, which was kept by Alpheus Bullard, on Broad street, in the north part of the village where the widow Cox now resides. It had been used as a storehouse by the public,and probably as early as the Revolutionary period. The war of 1812 did not materially detract from the settlement of this locality, and the population soon after rapidly increased, especially in the west part of the town where the mineral springs, by this time had become famous. Thereupon, in the year 1819, your territory was again divided, and the west half was organized into the town of Saratoga Springs, thus leaving the old town its present limits of about seven miles square. In the politics of the county, your town has borne no small part. Without including her former large territory even the small locality embraced within her present boundrries, has furnished members of the legislature of this state, viz: John B. Schuyler, A. D. 1795; Daniel Bull, 1800, and for two years; Jesse Mott, 1806, and for three years; George Cramer, 1816; Philip Schuyler, 1825; James Brisbin jr, 1832; Walter Van Veghten, 1838; William Wilcox, 1845; Henry Holmes, 1853; Samuel J. Mott, 1867. Besides those elected while residing here, many of her natives were promoted from other localities; for instance, Conrad Cramer was elected from Northumberland, in 1822, and more recently, Joseph W. Hill, from Saratoga Springs, in 1871. John Cramer, who removed to Waterford about the year 1800, was frequently elected to assembly and senate, and twice to congress. It has been truly said of him that he exerted more political influence in his locality, taking the number of years into account, than any other man of his time. John B. Brisbin, a native of this place, also has been a senator from Minnesota, and, if time would permit, many others might be mentioned who have become conspicuous in official positions in different sections of the union. Time, and the spirit of the American people to move forward into new fields of enterprise, have, here as everywhere, worked mighty changes. Of the men who were in our army under Gen. Gates, in the great campaign of 1777, we do not find the descendants of but four now residing in this village. One, the family of George Strover, who was a son of John Strover, before mentioned. Second, the family of the widow of Doctor Oliver Brisbin, a grand-daughter of Col. John Ball, who was a lieutenant in the campaign, and a distant relative of Gen. Washington. Third, Gordon and Charles Van Volkenburgh, the former of whom yet preserves the musket carried by his grandfather, Lambert Van Volkenburgh during that eventful campaign. Fourth, captain and afterwards major Hezekiah Dunham, before mentioned, the ancestor of Samuel Wells, esq., J. H. Dillingham, and other residents of this village. There are many other residents here who had ancestors in the army of the revolution, but they did not serve in the campaign of 1777, in this locality, so far as we have been able to ascertain. Of the patriots who served in the war of the revolution, none remain. Of those who served in the war of 1812, but two now reside in your village, William McCreedy and George Strover; the former of whom to-day, with elastic step, walked in your procession.

Time has worked mighty changes in human events. For a century and a half this county was the theatre of the contest between the protestant English and catholic French forces of the religious world. By the fall of Quebec and the peace of 1763, with the aid of our people, the British became master of this continent. After the surrender of Burgoyne in 1777 that same catholic French nation, joined us in the struggle against the British empire, and with their aid, we established a nation where religious freedom is secured to all mankind. Hence as a result we have this day witnessed the pleasing spectacle of a procession of Sunday school children, in which the protestant and catholic have marched through your streets under the stars and stripes in beautiful harmony. Thus an all wise Providence overrules the ambitions of men for the benefit of the cause of progress and righteousness.

One hundred years ago our colonies had less than three millions of people, while now it has over forty, and is one of the most powerful nations on the globe. Then the district of Saratoga, comprising one-third of the present county, did not exceed 2,000 inhabitants. Now the same territory contains 30,000 living souls. Then the locality of seven miles square, which forms the present town, had probably less than 300, while the census of last year shows a population of 4,392. Then this beautiful elevation north of Fish creek, had less than a score of inhabitants. Now it has two villages and over 2,000 intelligent freeman, with the prospect of being a numerous city, in the early future. Then the soil, wild and mostly uncultivated; now blooming like the rose, and affording abundance of grains and fruits to make glad the heart of civilized man. Then the streams located here by a beneficent Creator, were running to waste. Now, harnessed by man's intellect, they are doing the work of a thousand hands. Then the fort and the army demanded the exertions of the public. Now the arts of peace are flourishing around us, while the education of our children and the development of the races demand the best thought of mankind. Then the romance and horrors of war were familiar to every ear. Now we feel confident that those days have gone by forever, so far as our people are concerned, and the time is now here when we can safely "beat the sword into the plowshare, and the spear into pruning hooks." Had the wildest enthusiast one hundred years ago predicted the great nation of power, of civilization and intelligence, that July 4, 1876, would witness on this continent, he would have been called a madman. Twenty years ago if any such enthusiast had predicted that, on this day the stars and stripes would float over a nation, free without a slave, he certainly would have been counted unfit to manage the ordinary affairs of life. Yet, that time foretold by the Prophet Isaiah has come, when every man in our country, can plant his own vine and eat of the fruit thereof. And, to-day, the praise and prayer of forty millions of happy people unite and are ascending in thankfulness to God for the manifold blessings won for them by the patriotism of their fathers. It dwelling so fully upon the terrible tragedies of the past we do not intend to concede that such an age is to be held up as a model for future generations; on the contrary we believe that the parent or child who speaks the truth, deals justly, performs his duty, and dares to do right, will be a saint, exalted in heaven far above the Cæsars and Napoleons, made famous upon the records of human history. You are justly proud of your old Saratoga, of its hills and valleys, its patriotic and intelligent people, and of its historic fame. So long as man continues to love the truth and do the right, will the government, by the people, and for the people, declared an experiment one hundred years ago, continue to be a success, to protect and bless mankind through the centuries of the great future.

www.ingramcontent.com/pod-product-compliance
Lightning Source LLC
LaVergne TN
LVHW011144110826
845150LV00008B/2496
* 9 7 8 1 4 1 8 1 9 2 7 4 7 *